Herbert Andrews Powell

Lyrics of the White City

Herbert Andrews Powell

Lyrics of the White City

ISBN/EAN: 9783744775359

Printed in Europe, USA, Canada, Australia, Japan

Cover: Foto ©Thomas Meinert / pixelio.de

More available books at **www.hansebooks.com**

LYRICS

OF

THE WHITE CITY.

BY

HERBERT POWELL.

LONDON:
SIMPKIN AND CO., LIMITED, STATIONERS' HALL COURT, E.C.

WINCHESTER:
WARREN AND SON, PRINTERS AND PUBLISHERS, HIGH STREET.
—
1896.

INSCRIBED

TO THOSE HER CITIZENS, WHO KNOW THE PRIVILEGE

OF A BEAUTIFUL INHERITANCE.

H. P.

.

CONTENTS.

CONTENTS.

LYRICS OF THE WHITE CITY.

A DEDICATION SONG.

Sun of a summer day,

Myriad suns of the night,

Look on the measures of love, that I lay

Here in the eye of your light :

Song that would spurn the dust ;

Song of my heart that would soar to the height

Crowned of an ancient trust.

City ! thou maid sublime,

Heart of a people's esteem,

Dowered of graces that quicken with time,

Soul of a craftsman's dream ;

Liege of unmeasured love ;

Bathed at thy feet by the steadfast stream,

Clasped by the hills above :—

Hills that are sternly set,

Fastness and fortress to guard,

Staunch in the strength of the years that beget

Pride in your peerless ward ;

Silent with song unsung ;

Hills ! at her birth that were century scarred,

Hills ! in her prime yet young :—

Stream ! that art wholly meet
Ever her handmaid to be ;
Honoured to carry the cup to her feet,
Blithe to be held in fee ;
Plying thy gleaming skein,
Threading a silver embroidery,
Wrought in her emerald train :—

Man ! that art manhood's heir,
Forged in the chain of the years ;
Heir to the fruits of the toil and the prayer
Wrung from the builder-seers ;
Man ! that inheritest
Stones, that they fashioned in laughter and tears,
Gift of their manhood's best :—

Guardians of the day,

Watchmen, aware of the night,

Charged of a jewel of eloquent ray,

Soul of the city white :

Fain of her sovereign name ;

Fanning the torch of devotion alight

Unto a purer flame :—

Take of my heart a song,

Heart that is fain to be bold,

Heart that would arm to the challenge of wrong,

Song that would praise the gold,

Song that would spurn the dust,

Song that would soar to the hearts that uphold

Truth in a loyal trust.

LYRICS.

I.—OF THE CITY.

A CITY OF MEMORIES.

———

My window looks upon the street,
  The city's voices gathered there,
Stream in for ever, and the beat
Incessant of incessant feet
  Pants upward through the vibrant air.

A thousand cries are in the stone,
  But one note rings upon the ears ;
Change treads a measure of its own,
But through it runs an undertone,
  The pulse of the continuous years.

And fancy wrapt me in a trance,

  A day-lit dream of parted lids,

And crowned the head of circumstance

With halos of a high romance—

  Fancy that bids not nor forbids :

Led backwards past the later light

  To where the legend-moon, hung low

In skies of fable, freed the night

Of darkness to a mystic sight

  Of visions in its amber glow :

Where meads, rude Time hath over-built,

  Were mantled in the sanctity

Of joust for knighthood, and the tilt

At shame, the single heart, the lilt

  Of the high song of Chivalry.

And wholly fair and half divine
　The incense that encompassed me ;
Till fancy barred the inner shrine,
And lightly crossed the purple line,
　Where legend clears to history.

The sun that smote the casement-pane,
　Mirrored the flash of sun-smit helm,
When men rode out to meet the Dane,
Or spurred victorious in again
　With safety for a shaken realm.

The shout from yonder playing-field
　Swelled to a hoarser triumph-shout,
When instant battle rocked and reeled,
And the cry rose, "they yield, they yield"—
　The inch that grew an army's rout.

The bells, whose dim confusion rolled
   And tenfold from their echoes grew,
Rang to a home of kings, and tolled
The latest journey of the old,
   Or crashed a welcome to the new.

.   .   .   .

And dream on dream held pictured sway,
   Until the voice I hold most sweet
Sped yesterday upon its way
Unmourned, and bade a bright to-day
   Look through my window from the street.

SUNRISE.

———

Lo ! all the life of all the world
  Is flushed across the east ;
From Dawn's high altar, richly pearled,
  The lark, her tuneful priest,
    His service owns,
    While he intones
Her matins to earth's greatest and her least.

One trembling shaft, Dawn's messenger,

Lights on the eastern crest,

And glances quivering to the spur,

That fronts it from the west;

And passing smites

The storied heights

Of tower and turret to the day's unrest.

Deft morning throws athwart the dale

Her shuttle, nothing loth

To weave a white and clinging veil,

And hide the servile growth,

That basely crawls

'Neath nobler walls,

The barren mildew of a later sloth.

Behold the day-king, full astir

   In royal opulence,

Kindle the mystic gossamer

   To an unseen incense,

      And princely rise

      Through breathless skies

In splendour to his noon-day audience.

FAIRY NOON.

———

COME unto the eastern height;
   Queenly rides the moon
In the zenith of the night:
Midnight by a fairy sleight
   Charmed to fairy noon.

I will take thee by the hand,
   Point thee to the west;
At our feet a fairyland
To the waving of my wand
   Dimly manifest.

Seize upon yon silver beam,
  Hold its magic floss;
I will spirit thee o'erstream,
Where the minster in a dream
  Clasps its sacred Cross.

Thorough flying buttresses
  Winking planets peep
At the graven memories,
Under shadowed canopies
  Wakened from their sleep.

Upwards, whence the owl hath flown,
  Airily we'll climb,
Where the fairies' toil hath sown
Yellow lichens on the stone
  At the nod of Time.

Where the laughing gurgoyle hears
    Niche and angle worn
At the bidding of the years
By the silent pioneers,
    Till the blush of dawn.

Follow me to Wykeham's school,
    Force the midnight gate ;
Watch the fairies scattering wool,
Where the scholar and the fool
    Daily congregate.

I will lend thee magic wings
    Up the tower to win,
Where a host of chattering things,
Yesterday's imaginings,
    Sit apart and grin.

We will hover, and be lost,
　Where the spangled motes
Flicker upward elfin-tost ;
　Where deep shadows are embossed
　　'Neath the gurgoyles' throats.

Be thou still my wanderer,
　Where, from scholar life,
Heard the kingly chronicler
From afar a muttered stir
　Of the Danish strife.
　.

Phantoms of their sunlit selves
　Flash the shadowed halls ;
And a nimble band of elves
Dances, frolics, spins, and delves
　'Mid the silvered walls :

Walls with elfin characters
　　Delicately traced;
Buttresses, and carven spurs,
By the small artificers
　　Lovingly defaced.

.　　.　　.　　.　　.　　.　　.

List! it is the mavis' tune,
　　List! and come away;
Droops apace the westering moon,
Faints the fairy afternoon
　　In the world of day.

THE FLOWERS ON HER WALLS.

———

FLOWERS are bright about thy feet,
   Flowers have climbed thy walls,
Wanton in their sure retreat ;
   And, whate'er befalls,
From their vantage-ground defy
All the seasons' armoury.

Tiny tendrils of the spring
   Knit a fairy lace,
Busily a-wandering
   O'er a barren face ;

Charming January's grey
To the emerald garb of May.

Gilliflowers enriched of May
   Crave a royal boon,
Spend a fragrant month, and pay
   Golden debt to June
At thy feet, and wither there,
Jetsam of the tides of air.

And it happened on a day
   By the wind uplift
Fell a little seed astray
   In a stony rift;
Judged thy minster wall amiss
For an age-worn precipice.

Sprang a red valerian,
   Finding ample store
By a potent talisman
   O'er the minster door ;
Wore a blush the summer round
That it trod on holy ground.

Summer's treasuries are spent,
   Winter doth emboss
Nodding dingle, golden bent,
   On thy walls with moss,
By the scythe of April shorn
To a trim and velvet lawn.

Passion have they to confess,
   But nor voice nor lute ;

Yet they love thee not the less
  That their love is mute :
Leaf to flower, and flower to seed,
Silent homage still they plead.

Music is love's honey'd breath,
  Song is ever free ;
Ancient glory lingereth
  Round thy stones, and we
Breathe the breath of thy repute,
Love thee, and may not be mute.

TO WILLIAM OF WYKEHAM.

DEATH is no thirsty sea, whereto life's buoyant
stream descending
Loses in viewless vastnesses the current of its
aim ;
Death is no hungry pit, that hath unutterable
ending
In blackness for the brightness and the quick-
ness of life's flame.

The life, that slides from spring to sea, and swells
and gathers motion,
Breaks on the harbour-bar of death into a
thousand ways,
A thousand glancing threads, that braid the texture
of an ocean,
Shot with the lights of other lives across its rest.
less maze.

And evermore soft wave-born airs at twilight, land-
ward breathing,
As sighs for things remembered, to the purple
foreshore press,
And break upon the cliff to countless filaments
enwreathing
The living things of their desire, that bend to
the caress.

Master ! where once thy feet trod prints, thy
    homing spirit lingers,
  Breathes in the night-winds' harmonies, fast
    thronging from above,
And with the clinging touch of unforgotten passion
    fingers
  The stones that are as lodestones to the spirit of
    thy love.

The wine of life brims ever o'er the cruse of thy
    bestowing ;
  The seed-time of thy hopes has worn to harvests,
    that have been
Seed-times for later harvestings ; and streams are
    full and flowing,
  Pledges of fairer fields through all the breadth of
    thy demesne.

The self-same golden light is flung from tower and
wall, repeating
The glory of the coming and the going of the
sun :
And pulses emulous of thine, that beat of old, are
beating,
And new hopes are as old hopes, for the old and
new are one.

Maker of men, and moulder of the manhood of
the nation,
Shaping the pliant years of clay true to their
noblest bent,
Great prelate, master-mason, prince of craftsmen,
thy creation
Of stone and of the lives of men shall be thy
monument.

LYRICS.

II.—OF HER MINSTER.

THE MAKERS OF THE MINSTER.

A COFFIN for their bones,
And marble for their memory;
But the clear voice of living stones
For their eternal eulogy.

Great heart of greater man!
Albeit a narrower world they trod,
They needs must have an ampler span
To house their homage to their God.

Nor all their suppliant pride
Could frame a canopy too high,
Nor walls from aisle to aisle too wide
To echo back their litany.

Not for their own brief hour
Of life they added length to length,
But gave their stones enduring dower,
A thousand conscious years of strength.

Theirs was a rare control,
That knew the measure of its own ;
A purpose that inlaid its soul
Bonded in courses with the stone.

From line to line they wrought
The imagery of their heart ;

To springing arch and pillar taught
The fabric of their nobler part.

And we, who blindly tread
Small foot-prints down a broader age,
May marvel with uncovered head
How greatness burst its meaner cage.

How like a trumpet-blare
The organ's clarion chant is cast
Triumphant, while the captive air
Thrills with the passion of the past.

The listening aisles resound,
As echo unto echo saith,
That here a nation's spirit found
Fit record of a nation's faith.

Still is the fire aflame ;

The fuel of their lives unspent ;

The spirit of their single aim

Breathes through their peerless monument.

A coffin for their bones,

And marble for their memory ;

But the clear voice of living stones

For their eternal eulogy.

MINSTER BELLS.

——

RING, bells, a clamorous peal ;

The eager world shall reel

With throbbing waves of life flung on mankind ;

A storm of triumph ring,

Tempestuous challenge fling,

The years that wait have ears, though they be
blind ;

Peal ten exultant notes

From ten tumultuous throats

Together down the highways of the wind.

But hark ! a muffled chime,
An echo rung from Time,
Whose finished years are built into a wall ;
A whisper faintly cast
From barriers of the past,
Where tides of outlived passion heave and fall ;
A sob, a sigh, a tear,
To greet the unconscious year
With tidings of its kin beyond recall.

Soft, soft, ye other nine ;
A life's unravelled twine
Has sundered been by fate's impatient knife ;
Death's single song be sung
By one loud iron tongue,
The unison of sorrow following strife ;
The measure of his dirge
Falls as a ruthless scourge
In blows, that mark the issue of a life.

EVENSONG.

—

THE radiant windows were aflame
In sunset splendour, spread
And shivered in the mullioned frame
To rainbow fragments, shed
In crimson stain
And amber rain
On sacred memories of the dead.

Divinity, that never dwelt

In temples made with hands,

Writ on the golden mist, and spelt

The glory of all lands :

A mystic glint,

A hallowed print

Of a dim presence on the sands.

Prayer, as a steady taper-fire,

Pointed its upward flight ;

A wistful breath of rapt desire

Charged the full air, to light

By urgency

Of suppliant knee

The sacred presence into sight.

One magic voice interpreted
A sore world's mute unrest,
Then as a flashing river sped
Hope to the bitterest;
And bared the core
Of grief, and bore
The burden on its healing breast.

An echo from the full choir's heart
Answered the silver phrase;
The harmony of part with part
Wrought a melodious maze
From right and left,
The warp and weft,
Unto the perfect web of praise.

From bay to bay reverberant rolled,

Striking rich answers there,

An amen echoing sevenfold :

And silence born of prayer

Hovered among

The kneeling throng,

And wore a larger reverent air.

Fair evening dropped a tremulous lid

Across the eye of day ;

The vaulted canopy was hid ;

And vision fell astray

On tower and tomb,

Where a deep bloom

Spread by the herald twilight lay.

Night from the roof's dim labyrinth

   Her falling tresses shook,

Made mystery of shaft and plinth,

   And softly overtook

      From stage to stage

      The graven page

Chiselled upon Death's marble book.

SUNSET.

———

THE western doors were wide,
Flung widely to the western sky,
　Whose radiant majesty
Beat on the niched and fretted fane,
Beat, and was beaten back again.
The master-builder, crimson-browed,
Gazed ever at the pageantry,
　That blazed abroad and filled
The purple lattice of the cloud.

The whispering limes distilled
A fragrant air, and softly vowed
To the entreaties of the winds
 An amorous secrecy.

And one enchanted bird
Aloft melodiously rejoiced
In song that mounted nigh and nigher
The heart of Heaven, the fount of fire:
And all the subtle air was voiced
And busy with faint harmony,
That dropped bewilderingly among
The expectant strings of memory,
 And gathered into song.

. . . .

Wide are the gates of the western sky,
 Wider and wider flung ;
Banners of gold from yon armoury.
 Purple and gold, are hung.

Realm beyond realm of a larger state
  Glow through a crimson rift ;
Pomp of a princelier potentate,
  Barred by the level drift.

Winds ! in your wayward wanderings
  Searching the roof of the globe,
Sweeping the fringe of the golden wings,
  Hem of the purple robe ;

Unto the gates of the West presume,
  Stoop in a soft anthem ;
Win me to earth but one golden plume,
  Thread of the purple hem.

Clouds ! in your myriad multitude
  Lit by the jewelled crown,
Pause in the path of your vagrant mood,
  Passing the glory down ;

Up in the wake of the winds, aspire,
   Lifting my whispered claim ;
Win me a flash of the hidden fire,
   Touch of a purer flame.

Lark ! of thy gift of a minstrel sense,
   Largess of suppliant song ;
Lark ! of thy musical eloquence,
   Enter yon hidden throng ;

Pour at the feet of the majesty
   All thou hast ever sung ;
Win me a glimpse for a clearer eye,
   Song for a richer tongue.

.   .   .   .

  So ceased the rhythmic spell :
Across the west unsparing fell
A crescent shadow, that prevailed

Against her panoply ;
Slowly the vesper magic failed
In witchery over tower and tree ;
Died from the fane its borrowed gold ;
The lime-tops hushed their talk, to see
The master-builder's figure stoled
    In twilight drapery.

The restless winds subdued
Their frolic fancies, nestling deep
In flowery beds, and fell asleep ;
And sleeping dreamed, and dreaming wooed
A thousand honey-burdened throats
Their evening fragrance to disclose.
    The late lark's crystal notes
Sank in a cadence with the light ;
And silent from the east uprose
    The majesty of night.

SWITHUN'S LAMENT.

———

THREE times forty years have sped,
    Years of tranquil praise ;
Heaven above me, bend thy head,
    Weep for forty days.

Three times forty years of rest
    Under lowly stones
They have broken, to attest
    Relics in my bones.

Swithun, prelate Heaven-bid,
Priest of humble worth,
Covets not a place amid
Monarchs of the earth.

Fainer I they honoured me
In the tomb I prized,
Than exalt me thence, to be
Sainted, canonized.

Birds! to music set my plaint,
Winds! make ceaseless moan ;
Be attuned to my constraint,
Make my sorrow known.

Clouds! your founts of tears renew,
Sun! put on thy weeds ;

Flowers ! be pearled in mourning dew ;
　　Swithun 'tis, who pleads.

Moon ! in vapour veil thy head ;
　　Stars forbear to gaze ;
Tears of Heaven be gatherèd,
　　Weep for forty days.

.　　.　　.　　.　　.　　.　　.

Lo ! the Heaven above me hears,
　　Hears me and obeys ;
Weeps my lost and tranquil years,
　　Weeps for forty days.

FROM PRIORY TO DEANERY.

———

PRIOR of the Holy Rood !
   Give an ear to me ;
Who hast unto death pursued
Benedictine solitude
   In thy priory :

Holy Prior ! it was thine
   Ever to intone
From St. Swithun's jewelled shrine
Mass, and Vespers, and Compline,
   Terce, and Sext, and None.

Thine it was a blight to cast
  On thy brethren's bones ;
Weeks of penance, days of fast,
Nights of lamentation passed
  On the sorry stones.

They of turmoil undistraught,
  Drew devotion's breath ;
From a chastened spirit wrought
Visions, and from thought to thought
  Neighboured life with death.

Theirs to wrest the inner light
  From a darkened cell ;
Theirs the vigil of the night,
Theirs the body's sore despite,
  Till their passing bell.

E

Was it their true guerdon, Prior,
  Or their bitter loss ?
Didst thou chant high Heaven nigher ?
Didst thou scourge thy brethren higher
  Toward the Holy Cross ?

.   .   .   .

Prior ! was thy priory
  Planned in monochrome ?
Prior ! rise and come with me,
Learn the vivid scenery
  Of an English home.

Still more hoar the wonted walls ;
  Prior ! pass within ;
Voiceless are thy virginals ;
Hark ! how sweet the piano calls,
  And the violin.

Centuries have everywhere
  Trod a clear impress ;
Children's prattle in the air,
Felted footfall on the stair,
  Life and loveliness.

   .   .   .   .

Canst thou hear the nations tread
  Their quick measure, Prior ;
Pulses of the living sped
With the roll-call of the dead
  O'er a single wire ?

Canst thou mark a people's stir
  Down its steel roads hurled ?
Dost thou heed the constant spur ?
Dost thou hear in ceaseless whirr
  Hot wheels of the world ?

Prior, rest ! the busy sun
Watches from afar
Moaning tides of battle run
To a silence, only won
Through the din of war.

All our later day is rife
With an eager breath ;
Hearts are hungered for the strife,
And with the assault of life
Storm the gates of death.

LYRICS.

III.—OF HER NEIGHBOURHOOD.

HILL AND DALE.

TIME was when the great mother, Earth,

Or ever she gave mankind birth,

Wearied of her same station, set

In one subservience to the sun :

A single tremor of regret

Shivered her circle as she spun ;

And in a moment's space awoke

The pride of all her wheeling mass ;

With a majestic thrill she broke
The age-long bondage of her place ;
She leaned a little, bowed her yoke,
And bent another sunward face.

Then was her framework shaped anew,
Old order to disorder grew ;
The startled ocean from its bed
Flung a salt torrent, that was shed
O'er moor and forest, dale and fell,
And laid an everlasting spell
Of silence and unfathomed night,
Where days had wrought their fresh delight,
Where mid-land springs and summers smiled.
And stately mountain-tops were isled
And humbled by a hungry tide,
Where once in a sequestered pride
Massed legions of the clouds were piled,

The silent homage of the sky,
The ermine robes of royalty.

And as the serried armament
Of waters tossed a foaming head
For conquest of a continent,
New kingdoms from the ocean-bed
Leapt from their everlasting tomb
Of gathered death and endless gloom,
And lifted quivering on high
Stared blindly to an unknown sky.

Forthwith the face of all our land
Was tumbled in a thousand folds,
The naked framework of our wolds;
Then came the years with power to bless,
And in their train came laughing Spring
With flowers in her dainty dress,

Who paused, and fell to wondering,
And bade unloveliness grow fair ;
And Summer came, and trod the heel,
The dancing heel of winsome Spring,
And loved the labour of repair ;
And Autumn set her crimson seal
Of flaming leaf and ripened fruit
On the impress of Summer's foot.

And in a fuller time
A people, plucked from its own soil,
Braved seas to seek a fairer clime,
A land of promise for its toil.
And when they saw the morn unveil
The silver thread, that halves the dale,
The dale, that severs hill from hill,
They knew their pilgrimage o'ercome—
Hailed it a vision to fulfil

Hearts that were throbbing for a home.

Then stooping down a later gale,
That spread them over guardian seas,
An iron people, mailed and helmed,
Cast vulture glances, and o'erwhelmed
In clash of arms the ordered peace ;
Found, where the elbowed upland springs,
Meet throne-room for a line of kings ;
Saw her grow ever statelier,
Reared keep and bastion, and unfurled
A banner, that emblazoned her
A mistress city of the world.

What though her pomp be broken ? still
The flattering years repeat their tale ;
The seasons over stream and dale
Ply their bright trade from hill to hill.

Here is no torrent-cloven gorge,

No black chasm rent from mid-world forge ;

But an illumined open scroll

Of mossy hollow, velvet knoll,

Soft dimples, where the cradled wind

Whispers good-night, and wakes to find

Earth's mantle gemmed with diamond rime

From autumn tilth to lambing-time.

Behind the ploughman morn by morn

The furrow whitens with a drift

Of snowy sea-birds ; and the thorn

Puts shyly on its stainless shift ;

And lengthening days abundantly

Sift emerald dust upon the larch,

That points an April rainbow arch,

And shakes its scarlet tassels free,

And gives a gay good-bye to March.

The plover cries the summer in
With its feigned burden of a sin
Across a waste of ragged bent.
The linnet spends enraptured breath
In simple staves of long content,
Hymning his love, who broods beneath
The cloth of gold upon the whin.
The lark's song fades, and drops more nigh,
Drawing a bond 'twixt earth and sky
Of musical communion.
The streaming south wind riots on
Drunk with the passion it has won
From seas that sparkled to the sun ;
Flings upward as an unseen surf
The stinging incense of the turf,
And dances harping through the woods,
Mating with music all its moods ;
While over field and fell is played

The endless chase of sun and shade.
Embroidered hedgerows, week by week
Put other garlands on, that blow
And wither, till the scarlet glow
Lies vivid on October's cheek.

Here in this roofless unglassed fane
The ties of human brotherhood
Melt in a mist of solitude,
And dimmer sight unclouds again.
A limitless religion springs
In unconfined imaginings
Straight to the heart of hidden things,
Stripped of the vainer tricks of dress,
That cumbered all its singleness ;
And in a frenzy to be free
Drinks living draughts of liberty.
And broadening paths are lightly trod,

And airy feet are vision-shod,
And lost is all humanity
In the immensity of God.

TO ITCHEN RIVER.

———

I AM not often weary of the world,
    But thou art fair, so passing fair,
    That I could feign a deep despair,
To feel thy crystal-clear caresses curled
    About me in a love divine,
    And own my being wholly thine.

Thou wilt bewitch me from the walls I love ;
    There needs than thine no other call
    To bind me evermore thy thrall ;
I'll claim thy diamond wave my treasure-trove,

And find some magic to beguile
The largess of thy silver smile.

Thine is no passion of a wanton growth ;
    No winter access makes thee rave,
    No summer languor slows thy wave ;
But thine the surety of transparent troth,
    A constant heart that falters not,
    Within the steadfast hills begot.

Oh ! sweet adown the vale thy music swings ;
    And evermore, come night, come noon,
    When I o'erhear thy voice attune
The stones to cymbals and the reeds to strings,
    I shall entreat, again, again,
    The burden of thy low refrain.

Spell-bound we'll loiter 'neath the bridge, within
    The shadow of its solemn hush,

F

Nor heed the mad train's frenzied rush ;
We'll steal aside to shun the mill-wheel's din,
And smile to hear how vainly Time
Beckons us from some steepled chime.

We shall be greeted by the twinkling vole ;
Iris and spotted mimulus
Will squander golden smiles on us
Of friendship ; and we'll take a fragrant toll
From meadow-sweet, and briars that twine
With perfumed chaplets of woodbine.

The winds will stoop and play across thy face,
And ruffling jealously above
Will envy me thy dimpled love :
The halcyon, pausing in his radiant chase,
Will cleave the water to thy heart,
To commune with us all apart.

And when, above the sunset's amethyst,
 The sovereign moon through quivering space
 Finds her wan echo in thy face,
We'll bid the evening spin an opal mist,
 Through which no saucy star may peep
 And marvel that we do not sleep.

Of love or ruth thou wilt encrystal me;
 And so my body shall not die;
 We'll strike a truce, will Death and I,
We'll seal eternal compacts laughingly.
 Time on his single way shall go,
 And leave us in the ebb and flow,
The hymnal of the everlasting sea.

IN THE HOSPITAL OF ST. CROSS.

———

I PASSED within the gates, and laid
 My burden by ;
The bell tolled Vespers, and I prayed
 A sanctuary.

The world without of man and man
 Was torn in twain ;
I passed within ; the rent began
 To close again.

Sweet Mercy, with her flowery crown
    And brimming eyes,
And smiling Peace slid softly down
    The evening skies.

And Mercy at my side did stand,
    And took my scrip ;
And Peace divinely gave her hand
    Of fellowship.

Oh heart ! the sweet content to turn
    Life's latest page ;
To take the evening dole, and earn
    A toil-less wage :

To lie and watch a golden stream
    Flood dawn to day ;

To sit from noon to eve, and dream
My eld away :

To pass from peace to peace, and swell
The brotherhood,
That bartered faith for sight, and dwell
In God's green rood.

I would grow old, if age in me
Cometh to this ;
I would be poor, where poverty
Ennobled is.

A SONG OF ST. CROSS.

CALL, cushat, call !

The shadows are long ;

Croon over the wall

Thy cradle song ;

For sleep is the goal of the evening,

And cometh ere long.

Chime, belfry, chime !

For the silent dial,

Enamoured of Time,

Takes no denial ;

And the years, that are gathered and garnered,

Are mute as the dial.

Flow, river, flow !

The wide sea hath rest ;

And autumn shall strow

Sere leaves on thy breast ;

For the waters, that stirred in their noonday,

Are fain of their rest.

Hush, south wind, hush !

In a dream of peace ;

While the wan skies flush

To the day's release ;

For the day hath been dreamed to its twilight,

And the end is peace.